Bob Ross® Activity Book

50+ Activities to Inspire Creativity and Happy Accidents

Written by Robb Pearlman
Illustrated by Jason Kayser

RP | KIDS
PHILADELPHIA

Running Press Kids
Hachette Book Group
1290 Avenue of the Americas, New York, NY 10104
www.runningpress.com/rpkids
@RP_Kids

Printed in Canada

First Edition: June 2021

Published by Running Press Kids, an imprint of Perseus Books, LLC, a subsidiary of Hachette Book Group, Inc. The Running Press Kids name and logo is a trademark of the Hachette Book Group.

The Hachette Speakers Bureau provides a wide range of authors for speaking events. To find out more, go to www.hachettespeakersbureau.com or call (866) 376-6591.

The publisher is not responsible for websites (or their content) that are not owned by the publisher.

Text written by Robb Pearlman.
Illustrated by Jason Kayser.
Print book cover and interior design by Jason Kayser.

ISBN: 978-0-7624-7399-1 (paperback)

FRI

10 9 8 7 6 5 4 3 2 1

Introduction

Bob Ross was an artist, a teacher, and the host of a television show called *The Joy of Painting*. In each episode, Bob would talk to the audience and show them how to paint their own version of the picture at home. Bob encouraged everyone, no matter how old they were or how much practice they had, to use their imagination and to paint beautiful pictures for themselves. All the activities in this book are based on Bob's work and lessons and are designed to spark your own creativity. So, pick up a pencil, a crayon, or even a paintbrush, and have fun!

Finish the Picture!

Use the lines below to create a tall, snow-capped mountain.

Inspiration from Bob Ross

"Anytime you learn, you gain."

"You can do anything you want to do. This is your world."

Find Your Way

Help Bob's friend, Peapod the Squirrel, make it from deep inside
Bob's shirt pocket to peek out at our beautiful world.

FINISH

START

Answer on page 62

Sketch It!

Use this page to draw a meadow in the summertime.
Are there flowers blooming? Is the sun shining?

Use this page to draw the same meadow, but now
in wintertime! Is everything covered with snow?
Are there icicles hanging from the tree branches?

Cryptogram #1

Each of the numbers below corresponds to a letter (for example, in this puzzle, 7=T). Replace the numbers with their letters and you'll discover a phrase used by Bob Ross!

| 18 | 3 | 14 | 14 | 8 |

| 4 | 24 | 7 | 7 | 4 | 2 |

| 7 | 23 | 2 | 2 | 10 |

A	B	C	D	E	F	G	H	I	J	K	L	M

N	O	P	Q	R	S	T	U	V	W	X	Y	Z
						7						

Answer on page 62

Sketch It!

Use this space to draw your favorite kind of tree.
Is it an oak? A spruce? Is it big enough to
climb on or to build a treehouse in?

Dot-to-Dot #1

Connect the dots to find out what Bob has in his hand.

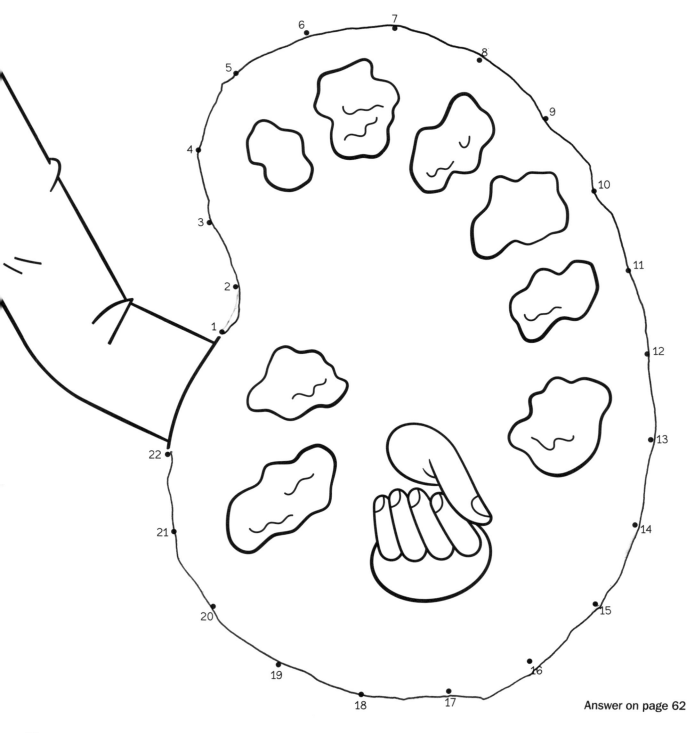

Answer on page 62

A Happy Little Crossword #1

Bob Ross's landscapes were inspired by his love of nature. The answers to this puzzle can be found in many of his paintings.

Across

2 Ground cover
4 Wide open space
7 Bigger than a hill
8 Large stones
9 Tall plant with branches
10 Bright and shiny

Down

1 Covers mountaintops
3 Out of the sunlight
5 Lazy water
6 Floating in the sky

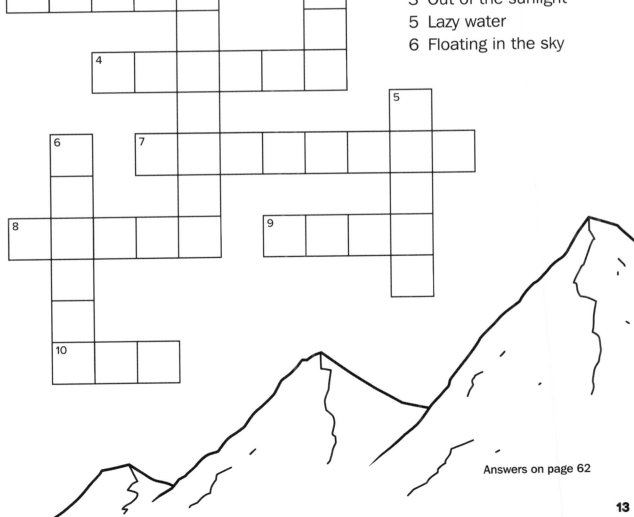

Answers on page 62

Sketch It!

Use this space to experiment with mixing colors.
What happens when you mix red and blue?
Green and yellow? Brown and orange?

Spot the Differences

Answers on page 62

Word Search #1

Bob often said that you needed the darkness
to show light. His paintings often reflected
opposing ideas or forces of nature. Search for five
pairs of words that seem to be opposites but can,
in fact, exist in the same painting.

```
L  S  S  S  H  L  E  O  D  T  K  T  T  O
D  G  R  O  U  N  D  O  M  A  S  A  I  O
E  R  I  A  R  T  L  R  T  I  L  U  L  D
W  N  O  A  T  L  K  U  O  R  O  K  U  Y
H  I  D  L  C  M  S  S  U  M  M  E  R  U
E  A  N  D  I  I  M  O  I  M  K  R  A  D
U  T  U  T  R  I  E  I  A  L  I  G  H  T
I  N  C  T  E  R  U  U  L  G  Y  M  S  S
K  U  D  L  A  R  W  N  I  I  N  D  G  R
U  O  A  M  O  R  N  I  V  L  R  Y  D  I
D  M  O  A  M  U  R  V  E  T  K  A  K  S
I  E  D  R  O  D  D  C  G  S  C  N  E  A
R  L  A  N  S  L  H  S  C  E  D  D  N  N
S  G  A  D  D  M  R  I  R  N  T  Y  N  A
```

sky
clouds
light
alive
winter

ground
mountain
dark
dead
summer

Answers on page 62

Finish the Picture!

Use this space to draw a picture of Bob Ross.

Word Jumble #1

Every artist needs the right tools to create. The words in this jumble
are some of the tools Bob used to paint his pictures.

aacsnv   canvas

eesla   easle

iptan   paint

rhbus   Brush

nipgnati eifnk ~~painting~~ painting knife

eltatep   palette

alrew   _____

oinmniiaatg   image mortion

a wrel
la wra

oinmm nii ajaat g

19

Cryptogram #2

Solve this cryptogram to find out what Bob thought
you could do. Here's a hint: 19=M.

7	11	18		14	6	13

19	11	12	5

19	11	18	13	20	6	10	13	22 |!

A	B	C	D	E	F	G	H	I	J	K	L	M
												19

N	O	P	Q	R	S	T	U	V	W	X	Y	Z

Answer on page 62

Sketch It!

Use this space to draw what you see out your own window.
Is it a street? Is it a farm?

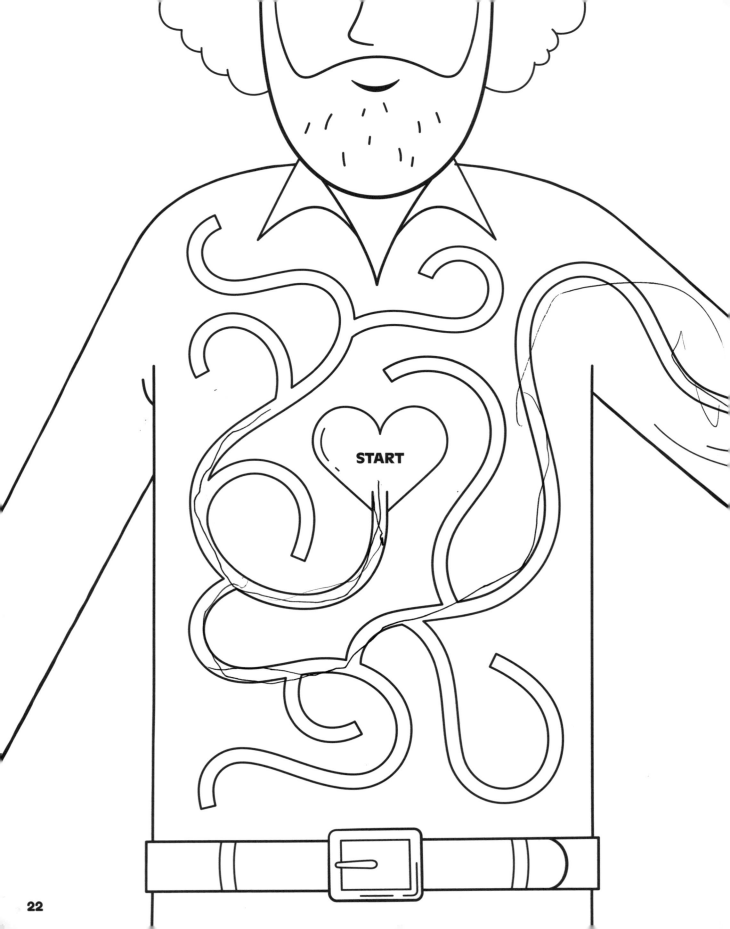

START

22

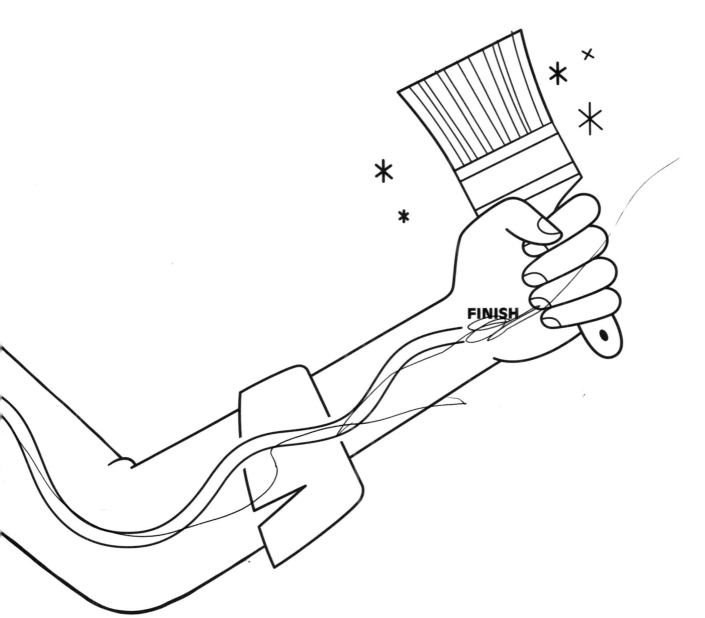

Paint Your Way

Paintings, or any artistic endeavor, come
from deep within an artist's imagination.
Can you help the idea for a painting travel from
Bob's heart to his paintbrush?

Answer on page 62

Word Search #2

Bob Ross loved nature, but he was especially fond
of animals. This puzzle features many of Bob's fuzzy,
furry, and feathered friends, some of which
even visited him on his show!

```
F  I  C  A  N  I  T  R  W  U  N  W  E  B
B  U  I  C  L  C  R  N  R  I  H  E  I  T
I  I  G  H  O  R  U  M  M  O  O  S  E  L
O  G  S  I  G  R  O  U  N  D  H  O  G  E
N  R  E  P  K  K  R  B  F  E  P  U  E  L
A  O  U  M  I  D  N  E  U  B  N  U  W  E
R  B  M  U  G  H  B  O  R  N  D  I  B  R
F  I  S  N  H  T  F  B  N  C  C  O  K  R
G  N  N  K  G  I  N  F  A  W  N  F  T  I
E  S  N  K  C  B  R  O  I  G  O  M  S  U
F  I  S  H  R  B  C  E  N  L  H  R  I  Q
O  W  G  I  A  A  B  I  W  N  C  A  L  S
A  N  E  M  N  R  U  O  N  B  S  A  Q  N
G  O  O  G  E  N  O  U  O  A  Q  R  A  I
```

Moose
Chipmunk
Crane
Robin
Squirrel

Owl
Rabbit
Groundhog
Fawn
Fish

Answer on page 62

Inspiration from Bob Ross

"Go out on a limb—
that's where the fruit is."

Sketch It!

Use this space to draw Bob's friend, Peapod the Squirrel.
What is Peapod doing? Eating nuts? Taking a nap?

Dot-to-Dot #2

Connect the dots to see who's sitting on Bob's shoulder!

Answer on page 63

Match It

Bob believed that friends were the most important things in life.
They matched up perfectly! Can you match up the object with its color?

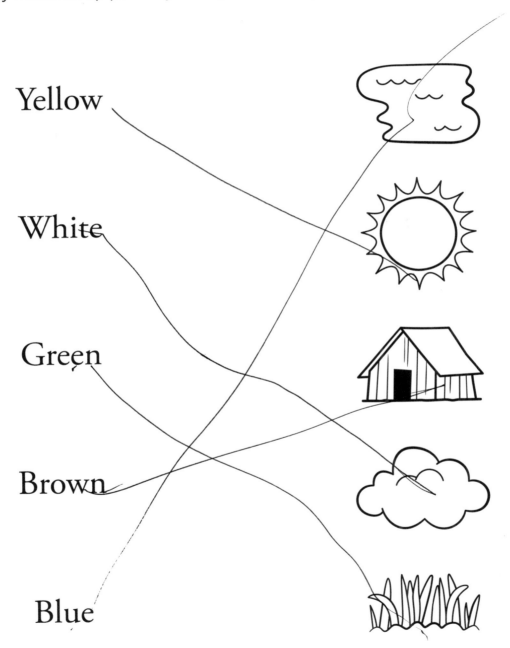

Yellow

White

Green

Brown

Blue

Answer on page 63

Word Jumble #2

Bob celebrated the natural world in his paintings and in his everyday life. Unjumble these words to discover some of the things he liked to feature in his landscapes.

teser   _____

uiantosmn   _____

uocsdl   _____

msarset   _____

oadwsme   _____

nscabi   _____

eksla   _____

ssubhe   _____

Answers on page 63

Finish the Picture!

Cryptogram #3

Solve this cryptogram to find out what Bob thought mistakes were. Here's a hint: 20=C!

8 14 19 19 16

14 20 20 7 25 22 21 17 10

A	B	C	D	E	F	G	H	I	J	K	L	M
		20										

N	O	P	Q	R	S	T	U	V	W	X	Y	Z

Answer on page 63

Happy Little Crossword #2

Bob Ross used the same thirteen colors in every one of his paintings. But by mixing them with each other, he created endless colors on his palette. The answers to these prompts uncover the full names of all thirteen colors.

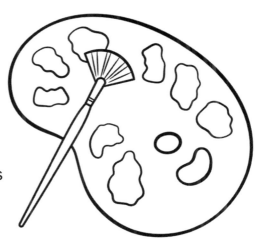

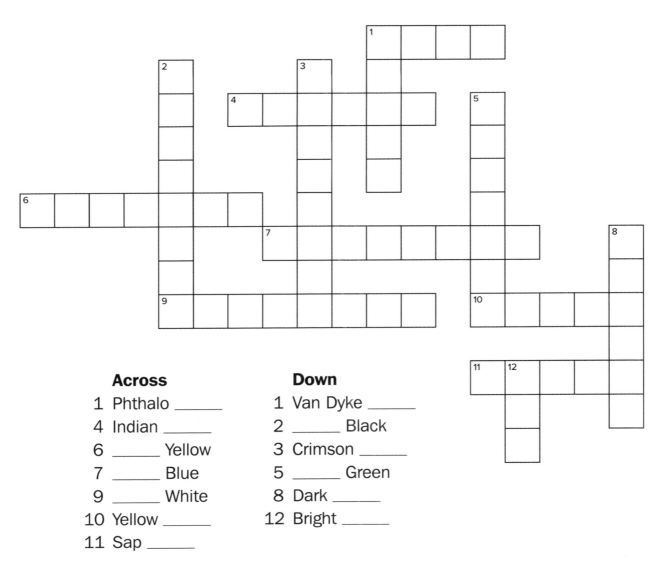

Across
1 Phthalo _____
4 Indian _____
6 _____ Yellow
7 _____ Blue
9 _____ White
10 Yellow _____
11 Sap _____

Down
1 Van Dyke _____
2 _____ Black
3 Crimson _____
5 _____ Green
8 Dark _____
12 Bright _____

Answers on page 63

Sketch It!

Use these pages to draw a picture of a lazy river.
What kind of fish swim in the water? What kind of plants grow in and
beside it? Are there any animals drinking from it?

START

Float Your Way

Many of the streams in Bob's paintings are filled with rocks and boulders that the water has to go around. Help this little boat make its way past all the twists and turns as it journeys toward the open sea!

Answer on page 63

FINISH

Spot the Differences

Answers on page 63

Word Search #3

Much like words are made up of an endless combination of letters,
Bob's landscapes are made up of an endless combination of paint colors.
Can you find some of his favorites in this puzzle?

```
R C R C N O W G B E U A Y O
N N E L E R A H L N O C C W
Y L D E C W S I W S H C E
O B Y O W E N L K T R N R E
L I O W L W E C E E E I I S
U A N N R W D I N L N K M A
I I L U L E K S O C O C S N
H N K L U R B O W R W A O N
N E D D W H R I N E L N E
R E B I I O M B O B R B R I
W E D S R E E L N W W O E S
I Y E L L O W N N R N N I W
I N B N R L I L G H W R Y E
C R R A Y E E N E E R G Y A
```

Green

Blue

Black

White

Sienna

Ochre

Red

Yellow

Crimson

Brown

Answers on page 63

Hide-and-Seek

Bob always said that there were no mistakes,
only happy accidents. So when a bit of paint was splashed
on his canvas or a brush stroke was too hard, he would hide
it with a rock, a bush, or even a tree! Can you find
the 8 objects hiding in this picture?

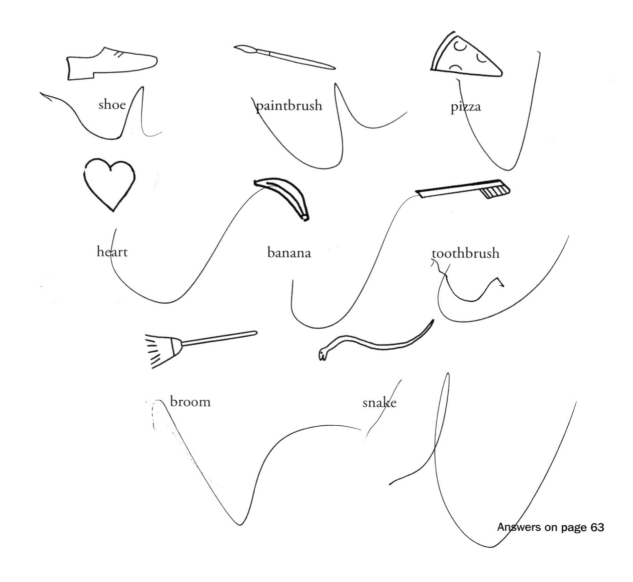

shoe

paintbrush

pizza

heart

banana

toothbrush

broom

snake

Answers on page 63

Sketch It!

Bob was able to finish a painting in 22 minutes on his television show. Can you finish a picture in the same amount of time?

Cryptogram #4

Bob knew how important friendship was, and nobody was more special to him than this little critter! Here's a hint: 3=R.

$$\overline{9}\ \ \overline{25}\ \ \overline{22}\ \ \overline{9}\ \ \overline{17}\ \ \overline{7}$$

$$\overline{18}\ \ \overline{21}\ \ \overline{25}$$

$$\overline{8}\ \ \overline{14}\ \ \overline{10}\ \ \overline{20}\ \ \overline{3}\ \ \overline{3}\ \ \overline{25}\ \ \overline{13}$$

A	B	C	D	E	F	G	H	I	J	K	L	M

N	O	P	Q	R	S	T	U	V	W	X	Y	Z
				3								

Answers on page 64

Happy Little Crossword #3

Bob Ross's quotes are almost as famous as his paintings. Solve these phrases to find out some of his most beloved sayings.

Across

1 Go out on a _____
3 Be a gentle _____
5 The Joy of _____
7 Let's get _____

Down

2 We don't make _____
3 This is your _____
4 _____ little trees
6 Isn't that _____

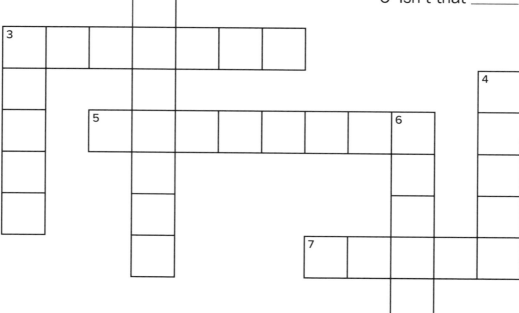

Answers on page 64

Inspiration from Bob Ross

"Don't forget to tell these special people in your life just how special they are to you."

Sketch It!

Use this space to draw whatever you like. This is your world!

Word Jumble #3

Bob was many things to many people. A lot of people think of him as an inspiration, or even as a celebrity. Unjumble these words to discover some of the titles he held.

pnteari   _____

createh   _____

torberh   _____

narveet   _____

hanubsd   _____

ertafh   _____

thos   _____

iefrnd   _____

Answers on page 64

Match It, Again!

Can you match the pictures on the left with what they go in, or on, on the right?

Fall Your Way

In nature, as in Bob's paintings, streams are often created when the snow on top of mountains melts and makes its way to the ground. Can you follow this snowflake's journey from atop this mountain down to the earth?

START

FINISH

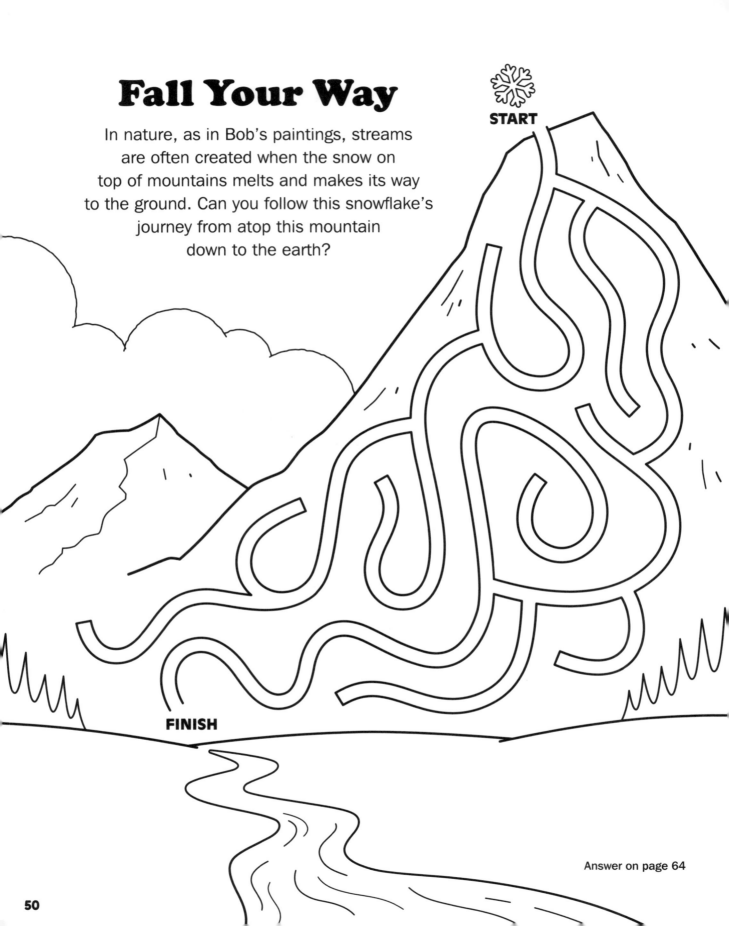

Answer on page 64

Dot-to-Dot #3

Connect these dots to see what Bob wrote
on almost every one of his paintings.

Answer on page 64

Spot the Differences

Answers on page 64

Word Search #4

Bob's television show, *The Joy of Painting*, brought his art to millions of viewers. Can you find the different elements that made his TV show possible?

```
A  V  M  S  H  H  P  O  A  E  O  H  A  T
E  H  H  B  P  H  O  N  G  O  A  M  N  M
N  E  A  P  V  E  L  A  E  N  E  I  R  H
O  S  A  E  O  R  S  M  I  S  A  T  I  P
H  R  L  U  S  H  T  A  N  P  S  C  P  V
P  V  B  N  O  I  S  I  V  E  L  E  T  A
O  E  V  N  B  E  A  P  T  N  I  S  N  V
R  A  S  A  T  E  T  T  E  L  A  P  T  A
C  S  E  C  C  O  S  I  E  T  S  C  C  I
I  E  H  A  M  A  I  P  E  N  T  E  C  H
M  L  S  M  T  A  S  V  V  C  H  S  R  P
A  R  U  E  T  B  I  E  E  O  G  E  A  N
T  G  R  R  N  H  H  H  S  G  I  H  A  A
A  E  B  A  N  T  E  P  E  P  L  E  S  E
```

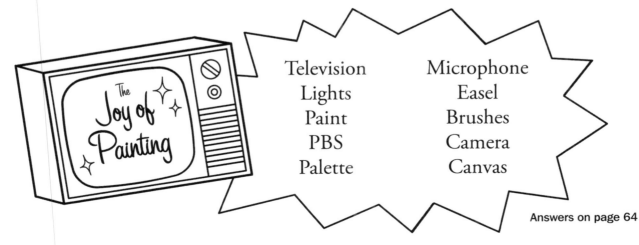

Television
Lights
Paint
PBS
Palette

Microphone
Easel
Brushes
Camera
Canvas

Answers on page 64

Sketch It!

Use these pages to draw a garden. Is it filled with flowers?
Maybe it has apple trees, pumpkins, peas, or carrots growing there?
Remember, this is your world, so you can even draw made-up
plants, trees, fruits, and vegetables!

Cryptogram #5

There are lots of colors in the world. Solve this cryptogram to discover one of Bob's favorites. Here's a hint: 13=L.

$\overline{}_{5}$ $\overline{}_{16}$ $\overline{}_{15}$ $\overline{}_{16}$ $\overline{}_{11}$ $\overline{}_{13}$ $\overline{}_{21}$

$\overline{}_{4}$ $\overline{}_{13}$ $\overline{}_{22}$ $\overline{}_{19}$

A	B	C	D	E	F	G	H	I	J	K	L	M
											13	

N	O	P	Q	R	S	T	U	V	W	X	Y	Z

Answer on page 64

Finish the Picture!

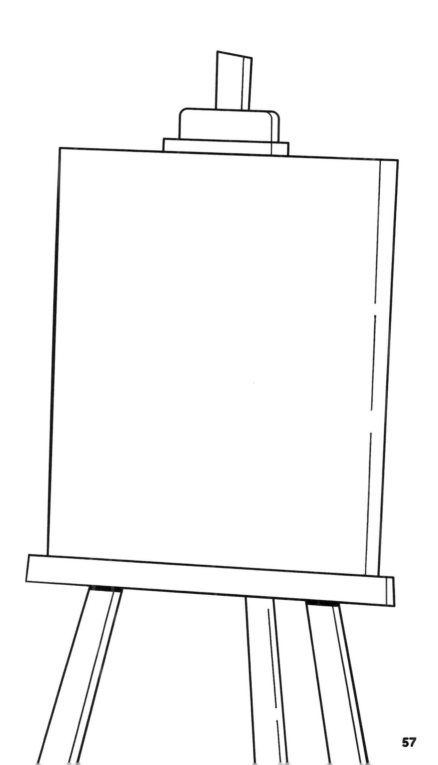

Sketch It!

Use both pages to draw your own landscape, just like Bob would!

Word Search #5

Bob's words meant just as much as his paintings. Try to find some of the words that are most associated with Bob Ross

C T M N A T U R E P S O I P
I M A G I N A T I O N T O M
A N O I T A R I P S N I G O
N A U R T T Y P P A H E R A
F G U T I F D N E I R F Y T
I P A I N T I N G A G T E N
R A L F I O I M N F U T A C
T I U M T T T P T A A R N E
B P A O O Y T I E I A N T N
A N R P H P Y B M I D H N O
I J T H P A O E A L P I M Y
N J N D N S J E M R A A G A
E I T R A T S R N E R C P T
R N I I H T E D A N I A B N

Inspiration   ~~Imagination~~
~~Painting~~   ~~Friend~~
Calm   Joy
~~Nature~~   Art
~~Happy~~   Beauty

Answers on page 64

Inspiration from Bob Ross

"The secret to doing anything is believing that you can do it. Anything that you believe you can do strong enough, you can do. Anything. As long as you believe."

"It's so important to do something every day that will make you happy."

Answer Key

page 10
HAPPY LITTLE TREES

page 7

page 12

A palette!

page 13

page 15

page 17

page 19
canvas, easel, paint, brush, painting knife, palette, water, imagination

page 20
YOU CAN MOVE MOUNTAINS

page 22
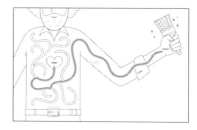

page 25

Answer Key

page 28

An owl!

page 29

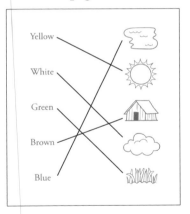

page 30

trees, mountains, clouds, streams, meadows, cabins, lakes, bushes

page 32

HAPPY ACCIDENTS

page 33

page 36

page 38

page 39

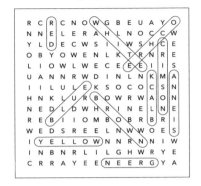

page 41

page 43

PEAPOD
THE SQUIRREL

Answer Key

page 44

page 48

painter, teacher, brother, veteran, husband, father, host, friend

page 49

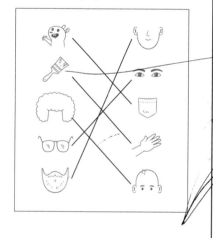

page 50

page 51

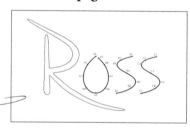

Bob's signature!

page 52

page 53

p. 56

PHTHALO
BLUE

page 60

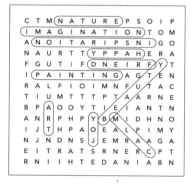